I can remember very clearly the day Michael Palin joined the Python team. Several of the original members had started to move on: Aneurin Bevan at the end of the second series, and Laurens Van Der Post shortly after that; now Graham Greene had told us that he wanted to do only six more shows. So we were understandably very cheered by the sight of Michael's smiling, affable, slightly squat figure entering the rehearsal rooms to meet us, and it was a matter of only months before he was officially invited to join.

And what an impact he immediately made! We were all thrilled to have someone so eagerly bustling around, shining our shoes, running out for cigarettes and making us countless cups of coffee. And what most people don't realise is that, in addition to all this, he wrote some of the material that was used in the television series and, if memory serves me right, even appeared in a couple of sketches as a performer.

In fact the only drawback with Michael was the noise. If he has a fault, and he definitely does, it is that he veers towards the loquacious. Many of us enjoy conversation: Michael likes talking. He just can't get enough of it. He's a one-man 24 hour radio news station without the musical breaks. In fact, in the early seventies he twice reached the semi-finals of the All-England Talking Championships. And I'm confident that he would have won a championship, had he not suffered the misfortune to compete in the same era as the legendary Alyce Faye Eichelberger. So after a few weeks we persuaded him to wear at rehearsals a kind of oratorical muffling device, constructed by Graham Greene from a gas mask and a handgun silencer, which enabled the rest of us to get on with our work.

Imagine my surprise then, when one morning I entered a silent rehearsal room, assuming Michael had not yet arrived, and saw him sitting in the corner reading a book, as quiet as an artichoke. It was as startling a sight as Chapman arriving on time, or Gilliam having an insight, or Idle doing charity work, or Jones not holding a strong opinion about something, or Greene playing ice hockey. I tiptoed across the room to see what book had affected Michael so dramatically, and I read on its cover the one word – 'Abroad'.

From the moment he put the book down the following day, he was hooked. The idea of abroad so fascinated him that from then on, he was almost always there, moving about it as much as possible, trying to find new bits.

So much so, that people speculated that this newly discovered wanderlust had displaced the old chatterlust. But it was not so; it was simply that Michael's constant wandering now presented him with the problem of whom to talk at. Fortunately this problem was neatly solved by his wife's suggestion that if a television crew were paid to accompany him he could rabbit interminably to them without the need, most of the time, to have any film in the camera.

As is well known, many of Michael's friends worried about this hyperactivity, despite the fact that it was giving his wife's eardrums time to regenerate; some felt it might mainly be a matter of diet, but I always believed it was psychological. So I decided to broach the subject with him, and, having chosen my moment carefully, I started by saying, 'Michael, a man can run and run for only so long but some day he has to turn round and face himself.' But already he was gone, off on another trip to cross Lake Titicaca on a pedalo. Thus were born *Around the World in 80 Days*, *Around the World in 79 Days*,

Around the World in 82 Days, and so on and so on and so on.
People sometimes ask me 'Will Michael settle down some day?'
Well, I sincerely believe he will. I can confidently see him, in another couple of decades, spending the day quietly driving round and round the M25, and then getting back home and putting his feet up in front of the fire to spend the rest of the evening with a good book and a TV crew. Let us hope that when this happens, his wife does not make the same error that she did last month when, coming across him in the bathroom, she called the police to report an intruder.

J.C.

Buenos Aires 1994

INTRODUCTION

Unlike the Spice Girls, the Monty Python team was formed by a triumph of unnatural selection. We were of many different heights, making group photographs tricky, and many different backgrounds – Graham Chapman had been a doctor, John Cleese a lawyer, Terry Gilliam a car mechanic, Eric Idle a Chelsea supporter and Terry Jones and myself the first to use the new toilets erected in Lambeth Walk, London in 1968.

The Spice Girls have another immeasurable advantage. They are naturally female. If the Pythons wanted to be female (which the work frequently demanded) we would have to engage in elaborate, often costly subterfuges, involving enormous padded brassières, reinforced high heels, shaved chests and make-up thick enough to disguise prodigious beard-growth. It's estimated that in portraying Mrs Thing on stage at the City Center, New York, Graham Chapman used over a ton of Revlon lipstick in an attempt to make Terry Jones laugh (and, less successfully, to try to become the New Face of Revlon).

In this little book I have trawled our work in an attempt to shed some light on the curious vagaries of history that threw people like us together and to see if there might be a lesson lurking here, a sign pointing towards some pattern for the future, a re-affirmation of the sublime ambition of the human spirit, a confirmation of the ineluctable destiny of mankind.

I came up with Knights who say "Ni", a Cheese Shop which has no cheese, a quiz for goats, a very long stage-direction and a song about a penis.

Sorry.

M.P. March 2000

ALL THINGS
DULL & UGLY

All things dull and ugly,
All creatures short and squat,
All things rude and nasty,
The Lord God made the lot.

Each little snake that poisons,
Each little wasp that stings;
He made their brutish venom,
He made their horrid wings.
All things sick and cancerous,
All evil great and small,
All things foul and dangerous,
The Lord God made them all.

Each nasty little hornet,
Each beastly little squid;
Who made the spiky urchin,
Who made the sharks? He did.
All things scabbed and ulcerous,
All pox both great and small,
Putrid, foul and gangrenous,
The Lord God made them all.
Amen.

STIG O'TRACEY REMEMBERS
THE PIRANHA BROTHERS

INTERVIEWER: I've been told Dinsdale Piranha nailed your head to the floor.

STIG: No. Never. He was a smashing bloke. He used to buy his mother flowers and that. He was like a brother to me.

INTERVIEWER: But the police have film of Dinsdale actually nailing your head to the floor.

STIG: Oh yeah, he did that.

INTERVIEWER: Why?

STIG: Well he had to, didn't he? I mean there was nothing else he could do, be fair. I had transgressed the unwritten law.

INTERVIEWER: What had you done?

STIG: Er . . . well he didn't tell me that, but he gave me his word that it was the case, and that's good enough for me with old Dinsy. I mean,

10

he didn't *want* to nail my head to the floor. I had to insist. He wanted to let me off. He'd do anything for you, Dinsdale would.

INTERVIEWER: And you don't bear him a grudge?

STIG: A grudge! Old Dinsy. He was a real darling.

INTERVIEWER: I understand he also nailed your wife's head to a coffee table. Isn't that true Mrs O'Tracy?

MRS O'TRACY: No, no, no, no, no, no, no, no, no, no.

STIG: Well he did do that, yeah. He was a hard man. Vicious but fair. *Vince Snetterton-Lewis agrees with this judgement.*

VINCE: Yes, definitely he was fair. After he nailed me head to the table, I used to go round every Sunday lunchtime to his flat and apologise, and then we'd shake hands and he'd nail me head to the floor. He was very reasonable. Once, one Sunday I told him my parents were coming round to tea and would he mind very much not nailing my head that week and he agreed and just screwed my pelvis to a cake stand.

KING ARTHUR
GOES TO SEE THE GALAHADS

ARTHUR KING *is in a rather smart mock-tudor suburban avenue. He has a paper and is looking at it and checking house numbers. He finds a house and goes up a long driveway to a large mock-Tudor house. Lots of spyholes, burglar alarms, barred windows etc.*
He presses the bell. A pause. Someone comes to the door. A bolt slides back. Then another and another and another, a key turns in a lock another bolt, then a key, two more bolts, then the door opens a crack on a chain. A rather opulent-looking upper-class twit peers out. He is restraining an enormous Alsatian. . . .

ARTHUR: Mr Galahad?

GALAHAD: Pronounced Ga'had, actually. Are you collecting for something, because I'd like to see some sort of official card, if you are . . .

WIFE *(off)*: Is it Jumble, darling? There's bags of stuff in the cellar.

ARTHUR: I'm looking for the Holy Grail.

GALAHAD: Ah wonderful, you saw the advert, then. Come in, come in. If you can just find your way through this bloody money . . .

GALAHAD *ushers* ARTHUR *into an opulent hall with a six-inch layer of banknotes everywhere.*

. . . that's the damn trouble of working in property . . . you amass such vast sums of loot that it's difficult to know where to put it. The cottage in Chelsea's being done up as a safe for when we're in town and we've bought a super little plot in Wales where we're going to sink a strongbox . . . then we can get rid of all this bloody stuff.

The scene ends with ARTHUR *being given a Holy Grail by the* GA'HADS. *They put it in a carrier bag for him and he takes it away.*

GOATS CORNER

Hello, goats! First a quiz:

Quiz

1. How many goats have stood for Parliament?

a) 1

b) 70

c) none

2. What animal can swallow a sheep whole?

a) a goat

b) an anaconda

3. Who was the famous Notts and England fast bowler who figured in the body-line controversy of the early 1930s?

a) Harold Larwood

b) a goat

4. Which goat wrote "Oliver Twist"?

a) Smokey

b) Billy Boy

c) Jacko

d) Tin-Tin

e) Not a goat at all

Answers

1. 70

2. an anaconda

3. Harold Larwood

4. Jacko thought up the title but *obviously* didn't write the book

Quotes about goats

What Famous People have said about Goats:

a) Milton: nothing

b) Robespierre: nothing

c) Dante: nothing

d) William Pitt the Elder: "I must go and put a goat on" (poss. misheard – Ed.)

e) Henry Ford: nothing

f) Clodagh Rodgers: nothing

g) Keith Miller (Great Australian all-rounder of the 1950s): nothing

Where to eat in London for Goats

a) Hyde Park

b) Regent's Park

c) Hampstead Heath

d) The Quality Restaurant, Tottenham Street

A message from Tonto

Once again it's been a bad year for goats, with humans confirming
their ascendency in the vital fields of politics, economics, education
and technological achievements. Only in the Arts and in the
mountains have goats maintained their supremacy. Eton, Harrow
and many other top public schools are still closed to goats, and, of
the Services, only the R.A.F. allows goats to take up anything other
than short-service commissions. Fashion still passes us by, and
when did you last see a goat on Top Of The Pops?
If we are to change this at all, we must learn to THINK GOAT. Don't
think of yourself as the plaything of Alpine milkmaids, the mascot of
the Irish Guards . . . Think of yourself as a GOAT. Don't be
compromised by the R.S.P.C.A. . . . remember GOAT IS GREAT!
Right on!
    yours *Tonto*

P.S. Do not eat this message

THE **HEALED LOONEY**

MOTHER: Well, how does it feel to be cured then?

SON: All right.

MOTHER: Your father and I spent a great deal of money getting you to Jerusalem.

SON: Yes. Thank you.

MOTHER: It wasn't easy for us you know. A lot of our friends didn't agree with what we did. I mean, we're not the sort of people to jostle around in crowds.

SON: No.

MOTHER: You were a looney you know. You were stark raving mad. You thought you were a bat.

SON: Oh?

MOTHER: Oh yes . . . you used to run around flapping and making strange high-pitched noises. You used to crouch on top of

cupboards and hiss at people.

SON: Oh.

MOTHER: Yes, you were very bad, wasn't he Miriam?

AUNTIE MIRIAM: Oh yes. *(She carries on laying out the cakes rather pathetically.)*

MOTHER: Well, maybe you'll be able to help around the house a bit now. Help your mother.

AUNTIE MIRIAM *hands around the cakes.*

AUNTIE MIRIAM: Jesus seemed quite a nice man.

MOTHER: Oh yes, very pleasant. We had a little chat about schools. *Suddenly the* SON *makes a strange high-pitched squeak. They all turn.*

MOTHER: What's the matter with you?

SON: Nothing Mummy, I just felt a little like a bat.

MOTHER: You didn't!

AUNTIE MIRIAM: Oh dear.

SON: Only a little. I just felt a little bat-like just for a moment.

MOTHER: *How* bat-like?

SON: Just for a moment I thought I was airborne again, winging my sightless way from eave to eave . . . that's all.

MOTHER: Well you're not a bat any more. Are you Paul? You *know* that.

SON: Oh yes, Mummy, but I still wish I was sometimes.

FATHER *enters.*

FATHER: How are you Paul?

SON: Fine, thank you Daddy.

FATHER *glances at* MOTHER.

FATHER: Well, good. Delicious cakes I must say, Auntie Miriam.

AUNTIE MIRIAM: I bought them in Jerusalem.

FATHER: Oh, well they're very tasty.

MOTHER *(sharply)*: Where are you going?

SON: I'm going to eat my cake up on the cupboard.

He pulls a chair over and starts to mount the cupboard.

MOTHER *(to FATHER)*: What did I tell you!

FATHER: Well, yes, but he is much better dear.

MOTHER: What d'you mean – *"better"*!

FATHER: Well, I mean there's not necessarily anything wrong in wanting to eat his cakes on the cupboard.

MOTHER *(voice rising)*: Of course there is you silly man! No rational, sane person goes and eats their cakes on top of a cupboard!

FATHER: Er . . . Paul. Paul!

The son is just climbing on to the top of the cupboard.

FATHER: Paul, why are you going to eat your cake on top of the cupboard?

SON: It's more comfortable up here, Daddy. Do you mind?

FATHER: Well, your mother and I would prefer it if you came and ate at the table with us.

SON: Oh, all right.

He gets down and comes over to the table.

SON: Is that what I used to do when I was a bat?

FATHER *(quickly)*: Well yes, you used to do some strange things, dear, but now it's all over.

SON: Oh yes, I don't think I'm a bat any more.

FATHER: No.

SON *(after a pause during which the atmosphere has relaxed a bit)*: It's funny really, both my parents being bats and me not being a bat. *(Father screams and throws a scroll at him)*

EGON RONAY'S GOOD PEOPLE GUIDE

41%   **Mr & Mrs Grayson**
Swindon
Wiltshire Map 24
19 Edworth Road
Swindon 262
First reports of this middle-aged couple were not good,
but since inclusion in the Guide last year their standards
have improved. Though Mr Grayson remains rather dull,
his wife is well worth a visit if you're in the neighbourhood.

69%   **Mr & Mrs Rogers, Brianette**
& Granny
Swindon
Wiltshire Map 24
21 Edworth Road
Swindon 701
A pleasant little family, Mr & Mrs Rogers are cheerful despite
financial difficulties and always good for a chat. Brianette is a well-
developed eighteen-year-old and Granny is deaf. Avoid the back
sitting-room.

80% **Doreen & Arthur Henbison**
Bletchley
Bedfordshire Map 36
6B The Flats
Bletchley 9041
At last what Bletchley has
lacked for years, a really
exciting couple. Arthur is an ex-
hypnotist, and Doreen in the
WAAF. They introduced wife-
swapping to the flats four years
ago and now it's hard to get in.
Must book – especially at
weekends.

18% **Mr & Mrs Potter**
Worthing
Sussex Map 18
88 Rockery Crescent
Worthing 204
An appalling couple, rude
and short-tempered. Their
kitchen is painted a
frightful yellow and Mr
Potter is an
uncompromising Marxist.

THE CHEESE SHOP

MOUSEBENDER: Now my good man, some cheese, please.

WENSLEYDALE: Yes certainly, sir. What would you like?

M: Well, how about a little Red Leicester?

W: I'm afraid we're fresh out of Red Leicester, sir.

M: Oh never mind. How are you on Tilsit?

W: Never at the end of the week, sir. Always get it fresh first thing on Monday.

M: Tish, tish. No matter. Well, four ounces of Caerphilly, then, if you please, stout yeoman.

W: Ah, well, it's been on order for two weeks, sir, I was expecting it this morning.

M: Yes, it's not my day is it. Er, Bel Paese?

W: Sorry.

M: Red Windsor.

W: Normally sir, yes, but today the van broke down.

M: Ah. Stilton?

W: Sorry.

M: Gruyère, Emmental?

W: No.

M: Any Norwegian Jarlsberger?

W: No.

M: Liptauer?

W: No.

M: Lancashire.

W: No.

M: White Stilton?

W: No.

M: Danish Blue?

W: No.

M: Double Gloucester?

W: . . . No.

M: Cheshire?

W: No.

M: Any Dorset Blue Vinney?

W: No.

M: Brie, Rocquefort, Pont-l'Évêque, Port Salut,

Savoyard, Saint-Paulin, Carre-de-L'Est, Boursin, Bresse-Bleue, Perle de Champagne, Camembert?

W: Ah! We do have some Camembert, sir.

M: You do. Excellent.

W: It's a bit runny, sir.

M: Oh, I like it runny.

W: Well as a matter of fact it's *very* runny, sir.

M: No matter. No matter. Hand over le fromage de la Belle France qui s'appelle Camembert, s'il vous plaît.

W: I think it's runnier than you like it, sir.

M *(smiling grimly)*: I don't care how excrementally runny it is. Hand it over with all speed.

W: Yes, sir. *(bends below the counter and reappears)* Oh . . .

M: What?

W: The cat's eaten it.

M: Has he?

W: She, sir.

M: Gouda?

W: No.

M: Edam?

W: No.

M: Caithness?

W: No.

M: Smoked Austrian?

W: No.

M: Sage Derby?

W: No, sir.

M: You do have some
cheese, do you?

W: Certainly, sir. It's a cheese shop, sir. We've got . . .

M: No, no, no, don't tell me. I'm keen to guess.

W: Fair enough.

M: Wensleydale?

W: Yes, sir?

M: Splendid. Well, I'll have some of that then, please.

W: Oh, I'm sorry sir, I thought you were referring to me, Mr
Wensleydale.

M: Gorgonzola?

W: No.

M: Parmesan?

W: No.

M: Mozzarella?

W: No.

M: Pippo Crème?

W: No.

M: Any Danish Fynbo?

W: No.

Camembert

M: Czechoslovakian Sheep's Milk Cheese?

W: No.

M: Venezuelan Beaver Cheese?

W: Not today sir, no.

M: Well let's keep it simple, how about Cheddar?

W: Well I'm afraid we don't get much call for it around these parts.

M: No call for it? It's the single most popular cheese in the world!

W: Not round these parts, sir.

M: And pray what is the most popular cheese round these parts?

W: Ilchester, sir.

M: I see.

W: Yes, sir. It's quite staggeringly popular in the manor, squire.

M: Is it?

W: Yes sir, it's our number-one seller.

M: Is it?

W: Yes, sir.

M: Ilchester eh?

W: Right.

M: OK, I'm game. Have you got any, he asked expecting the answer no?

W: I'll have a look sir . . . nnnnnnooooooooo.

M: It's not much of a cheese shop really, is it?

W: Finest in the district, sir.

M: And what leads you to that conclusion?

W: Well, it's so clean.

M: Well, it's certainly uncontaminated by cheese.

Dear Madame Palm,
I have a teensy problemette. As I was mincing down the road-poady the other Davy daykins, I saw an absolutely divine, but divine darling-heart!, jackety-poohs in ever so soft Sammy silk. Ooh! it drove me delirious ducky-darling, but when could I wear it?
The Rev. B. J. Mitchell,
Upper Choirboy, Gloucs.

Arson is a perfectly natural feeling, Geoffrey. How many of us at one time or another in our lives hasn't felt the need to set fire to some great public building or other. I know I have.

Dear Madame Palm,
I have a problem. You see I have bad breath. Also I am quite ugly. I am so embarrassed about this and I don't know who else to turn to for confidential advice. I am too shy to ask my family doctor and I would just die if anyone ever found out.
NAME AND ADDRESS SUPPLIED.
(Although in fact it is:

Betty Rogers,
32, The Cuttings, Bolton.
Telephone Number: Bolton 0123495)

Dear Betty, how many times must I keep telling you that sex is fun. I like it. You like it. Everybody likes it. Mr Robinson from the off-licence likes it twice.

27

THE **PROBLEM** WITH **SPANISH HOLIDAYS**

A would-be tourist explains his preferences to DEREK BOUNDER, *a travel agent.*

TOURIST: I'm fed up going abroad and being treated like sheep, what's the point of being carted round in buses, surrounded by sweaty mindless oafs from Kettering and Boventry in their cloth caps and their cardigans and their transistor radios and their "Sunday Mirrors", complaining about the tea, "Oh they don't make it properly here, do they, not like at home," stopping at Majorcan bodegas selling fish and chips and Watney's Red Barrel and calamares and two veg and sitting in cotton sun frocks squirting Timothy White's suncream all over their puffy raw swollen purulent flesh cos they "overdid it on the first day"!

BOUNDER *(agreeing patiently)*: Yes. Absolutely, yes, I quite agree . . .

TOURIST: And being herded into endless Hotel Miramars and Bellevueses and Bontinentals with their international luxury modern roomettes and their Watney's Red Barrel and their swimming pools full of fat German businessmen pretending to be acrobats and forming pyramids and frightening the children and barging into the queues and if you're not at your table spot on seven you miss your bowl of Campbell's Cream of Mushroom soup, the first item on the menu of International Cuisine, and every Thursday night there's bloody cabaret in the bar featuring some tiny emaciated dago with nine-inch hips and some big fat bloated tart with her hair Brylcreemed down and a big arse presenting Flamenco for Foreigners.

BOUNDER *(beginning to get fed up)*: Yes, yes, now . . .

TOURIST: And then some adenoidal typists from Birmingham with diarrhoea and flabby white legs and hairy bandy-legged wop waiters called Manuel, and then once a week there's an excursion to the local Roman ruins where you can buy cherryade and melted ice cream and bleedin' Watney's Red Barrel, and then one night they take you to a local restaurant with local colour and colouring and they show you there and you sit next to a party of people from Rhyl who keeps singing "Torremolinos, Torremolinos", and complaining about the food, "Oh! It's so greasy isn't it?" and then you get cornered by some drunken greengrocer from Luton with an Instamatic and Dr Scholl sandals and Tuesday's *Daily Express* and he drones on and on and on about how Mr Smith should be running this country and how many languages Enoch Powell can speak and then he throws up all over the Cuba Libres.

BOUNDER: Will you be quiet please.

TOURIST: And sending tinted postcards of places they don't know they haven't even visited, "to all at number 22, weather wonderful, our room is marked with an 'X'. Wish you were here."

BOUNDER: Shut up.

TOURIST: "Food very greasy but we have managed to find this marvellous little place hidden away in the back streets."

BOUNDER: Shut up!

TOURIST: "Where you can even get Watney's Red Barrel and cheese and onion . . ."

BOUNDER: Shut up!!!

TOURIST: ". . . crisps and the accordionist plays 'Maybe it's because I'm a Londoner'" and spending four days on the tarmac at Luton

29

airport on a five-day package tour with nothing to eat but dried Watney's sandwiches . . .

BOUNDER: Shut your bloody gob! I've had enough of this, I'm going to ring the police.

A corner of a police station. One policeman is knitting, another is making a palm tree out of old newspapers. The phone rings.

KNITTING POLICEMAN: Oh . . . take it off the hook.

PORT SHOEM
BY THE SPEVEREND ROONER

I've a grouse and harden in the country,
An ace I call my plown,
A treat I can replace to
When I beed to knee alone.
Catterfly and butterpillar
Perch on beefy lough,
And I listen to the dats and cogs
As they mark and they biaow.
Yes wature here is nunderful,
There is no weed for nords,
While silling by my windowflutter
Biny little tirds.

The Stratton Indicator

Permission to build new garden shed refused

Mr Leonard Whim (39), a local man, today attacked the decision of the Town Borough Council to refuse him permission to construct another garden shed near his £10,000 house in lower Ching, on the grounds that he already had one shed. 'This is worse than living in a communist state' Mr Leonard told one of our reporters. 'To my mind it's creeping socialism. I fought in the war for freedom to build garden sheds when and where you wanted.

Mrs Whim, 32, a trim, petite, blonde wearing a matching tweed costume in striking aquamarine with elegant lace-up boots, and a fiery rose hat, agreed, said a neighbour. Leonard Whim is well-known in the area and has two dogs.

A Councillor defended the decision amidst angry scenes outside the 17th Century 'Clatch', which is shortly to be demolished to make way for a new car-park. 'This whole thing' he said 'has been blown up out of all proportion. Although one or two members of the Council were quite frankly a little

unhappy about Mr Whim's plans to build a box-girder garden shed with split-level shopping piazza, covered walk-way, underground garage-cum-swimming pool, with facilities for all-night split-level shopping, and a split-level entertainment centre complete with bowling alley and split-level bingo hall.'

Press on

'I shall press on' said Mr Whim to journalists. 'I intend to convince the Council that they are wrong. This garden shed is going to be built, and when they see the Architect's presents I'm sure they will change their minds.' Mr Whim is head of a large road haulage firm and building works and has had many successful contracts with the Council.

33

WINNER OF THE LONGEST STAGE DIRECTION EVER

Long John Silver disappears. A pause. Two boxers appear. They circle each other. On one's head a bowler hat appears, vanishes. On the other's a stove-pipe hat appears. On the first's head a fez. The stove-pipe hat becomes a stetson. The fez becomes a cardinal's hat. The stetson becomes a wimple. Then the cardinal's hat and the wimple vanish. One of the boxers becomes Napoleon and the other boxer is astonished. Napoleon punches the boxer with the hand inside his jacket. The boxer falls, stunned. Horizontally he shoots off stage.

Shot of cat, watching unimpressed.

Napoleon does a one-legged pixilated dance across the stage and off, immediately reappearing on the other side of stage doing the same dance in the same direction. He reaches the other side, but is halted by a traffic policeman. The policeman beckons on to the stage a man in a penguin skin on a pogostick. The penguin gets half way across and then turns into a dustbin. Napoleon hops off stage. The policeman goes to the dustbin, opens it and Napoleon gets out.

Shot of cat, still unmoved.

A nude man with a towel round his waist gets out of the dustbin. Napoleon points at the ground. A chair appears where he points. The nude man gets on to the chair, jumps in the air and vanishes. Then Napoleon points to the ground by him and a small cannon appears. Napoleon fires the cannon and the policeman disappears. The man with the towel round his waist gets out of the dustbin and is chased off stage by the penguin on the pogostick. A sedan chair is carried on

34

stage by two chefs. The man with the towel gets out
and the penguin appears from the dustbin and chases
him off. Napoleon points to the sedan chair and it
changes into a dustbin. The man in the towel runs back on to the
stage and jumps in the dustbin. He looks out and the penguin
appears from the other dustbin and hits him on the head with a raw
chicken.
Shot of cat still unimpressed.
Napoleon, the man with the towel round his waist, the policeman, a
boxer, and a chef suddenly appear standing in a line,
and take a bow. They immediately change positions
and take another bow.
The penguin appears at the end
of the line with a puff of smoke.
Each one in turn jumps
in the air and vanishes.
Shot of passive cat.
After a pause, the cat gets up
and walks into the house.

MIDDLEWORD
BY E.F. GOD

When I created the world in those *amazingly* busy seven days, I remember it as being a tremendously exciting period. There was so much to do that I honestly had hardly any time to notice what I was creating. I know that sounds awful, but I think anyone who's created anything will realise that very often you become so tied up with whatever it is you're creating that you can't see the wood for the trees – and I was *creating* the wood and the trees!

I mean, some days were great. The first day, of course, we couldn't see a bloody thing. I mean, I actually had to invent light just so we could see what we were doing! Sounds crazy now, doesn't it! Once I'd got the hang of it and done the basics there were some very exciting moments, though. The firmament, which I did on the second day, was great because, to be quite honest, I had no idea what a firmament really was, I just had to have something to divide the waters from the waters, and it turned out to be just right for that purpose. I also liked the tree yielding fruit. I don't know, it just had a nice ring to it. I suppose, now, with the benefit of hindsight, perhaps I should have just stuck to the tree and forgotten the fruit, but I liked the fruit and I didn't know Adam and Eve would make such a bollocks of it (excuse my French). I've been quite criticised over the years for letting them loose in the Garden of Eden, but I gave them Free Will and they decided that rather than write poetry or sing to each or invent a board game they'd go and talk to snakes. All right, I accept that there was an inherent risk but honestly, if you could have the choice to do anything you wanted in the loveliest garden ever made, with rivers and trees yielding fruit all over the place, would you seek out the nearest snake and ask how you could best get a rise out of the park-keeper? The next thing is that poor old Muggins is being blamed for everything from the Black Death to setting fire to Windsor Castle. There is no evidence in any of my utterances that I tampered with the wiring in the Long Gallery, just below the little French satinwood side-table where the Queen keeps the telephone directories, and if you can find the phrase "And then God created buboes", then all right, I decimated Europe, personally, in the fourteenth century. (I mean, I *created* Europe in the first place, why would I want to decimate it?) Sorry to go on but there is a downside to being Creator (my capitals).

ISN'T IT AWFULLY NICE
TO HAVE A PENIS

NOËL COWARD: Good evening ladies and gentlemen. Here's a little number I tossed off recently in the Caribbean.

Isn't it awfully nice to have a penis,
Isn't it frightfully good to have a dong?
It's swell to have a stiffy,
It's divine to own a dick,
From the tiniest little tadger,
To the world's biggest prick.

So three cheers for your Willy or John Thomas,
Hooray for your one-eyed trouser snake,
Your piece of pork, your wife's best friend,
Your Percy or your cock,
You can wrap it up in ribbons,
You can slip it in your sock,
But don't take it out in public,
Or they will stick you in the dock,
And you won't come back.

THE ALL-ENGLAND SUMMARIZE PROUST COMPETITION

Showbiz music, applause, and ARTHUR MEE *appears from the back of the stage; he wears the now traditional spangly jacket.*

MEE: Good evening and welcome, or as Proust would say, "la malade imaginaire de recondition et de toute surveillance est bientôt la même chose". *(Roars of applause)* Remember each contestant this evening has a maximum of fifteen seconds to sum up "A La Recherche du Temps Perdu" and on the Proustometer over here . . . *(A truly enormous, but cheap, audience appreciation gauge; it lists the seven books of Proust's masterwork in the form of a thermometer)* you can see exactly how far he gets. So let's crack straight on with our first contestant tonight. He's last year's semi-finalist from Luton – Mr Harry Bagot.

BAGOT *in evening dress, comes forward from back of stage, he has a number three on his back.*

Hello Harry. You're on the summarizing spot. You have fifteen seconds from *now*.

BAGOT: Proust's novel ostensibly tells of the irrevocability of time lost, the forfeiture of innocence through experience, the reinstatement of extra-temporal values of time regained; ultimately the novel is both optimistic and set within the context of a humane religious experience, re-stating as it does the concept of intemporality. In the first volume, Swann, the family friend visits . . .

Gong goes. Chord of music, applause.

The meter has hardly risen at all.

MEE: Well tried, Harry.

VOICE OVER: A good attempt there but unfortunately he chose a

general appraisal of the work, before getting on to the story and, as you can see, *(close up of Proustometer)* he only got as far as page one of "Swann's Way", the first of the seven volumes. A good try though and very nice posture.

MEE: Now Harry what made you first want to try and start summarizing Proust?

BAGOT: Well I first entered a seaside Summarizing Proust Competition when I was on holiday in Bournemouth, and my doctor encouraged me with it.

MEE: And Harry, what are your hobbies outside summarizing?

BAGOT: Well, strangling animals, golf and masturbating.

MEE: Well, thank you Harry Bagot.

BAGOT *walks off-stage. Music and applause.*

VOICE OVER: Well there he goes. Harry Bagot. He must have let himself down a bit on the hobbies, golf's not very popular around here, but never mind, a good try.

MEE: Thank you ladies and gentlemen. Mr Rutherford from Leicester, are you ready Ronald? *(RONALD is a very eager man in tails)* Right. On the summarizing spot. You have got fifteen seconds from now.

RONALD: Er, well, Swann, Swann, there's this house, there's this house, and er, it's in the morning, it's in the morning – no, it's the evening, in the evening and er, there's a garden and er, this bloke comes in – bloke comes in – what's his name – what's his name, er just said it – big bloke – Swann, Swann . . .

The gong sounds.

MEE: Well ladies and gentlemen, I don't think any of our contestants this evening have succeeded in encapsulating the intricacies of Proust's masterwork, so I'm going to award the first prize this evening to the girl with the biggest tits.

The Stratton Indicator

Stratton go top of the League

By defeating arch-rivals neighbouring Cubsy by one run on Saturday Stratton go top of the Grisdale League, two points ahead of Sudsy and Wells. The main feature of their victory was a superb innings by local man skipper Hemsley who held off the Cubsy bowlers when the match seemed to be swinging their way. Details of the Match

Cubsy

Groat c. & b. Wilkes	0
Sprange l.b.w., b. Wilkes	1
Thompson J. run out	0
Caryotid P. st. Si, b. Rant	0
Flake c. Limp, b. Wilkes	0
Tickersley not out	
Watt J. l.b.w., b. Rant	0
Armstrong B. c. Rotter, b. Wilkes	0
Fletcher N. b. Rant	0
Thompson E. ht. wkt., b. Parkes	0
Extras	1
Total—All Out	

Stratton

Parkes b. Thompson	0
Si c. & b. Caryotid	0
Rant P. not out	0
Rotter b. Thompson	0
Limp rtd. hurt	0
Wilkes c. Watt, b. Caryotid	0
Cooke C. l.b.w., b. Watt	0
Cook P. b. Caryotid	2
Sampson R. st. Flake, b. Groat	0
Hemsley not out	1
Extras	
Total for nine	

THE ARCHITECT
SKETCH

CHAIRMAN: Gentlemen, we have two basic suggestions for the design of this residential block, and I thought it best that the architects themselves came in to explain the advantages of both designs. *(A knock at the door)* That must be the first architect now. *(MR WIGGIN comes in)* Ah, yes – it's Mr Wiggin of Ironside and Malone.

WIGGIN *walks to the table on which his model stands.*

MR WIGGIN: Good morning, gentlemen. This is a twelve-storey block combining classical neo-Georgian features with all the advantages of modern design. The tenants arrive in the entrance hall here, are carried along the corridor on a conveyor belt in extreme comfort and past murals depicting Mediterranean scenes, towards the rotating knives. The last twenty feet of the corridor are heavily soundproofed. The blood pours down these chutes and the mangled flesh slurps into these . . .

FIRST CITY GENT: Excuse me . . .

MR WIGGIN: Hm?

FIRST CITY GENT: Did you say knives?

MR WIGGIN: Rotating knives, yes.

SECOND CITY GENT: Are you proposing to slaughter our tenants?

MR WIGGIN: Does that not fit in with your plans?

FIRST CITY GENT: No, it does not. We wanted a simple block of flats.

MR WIGGIN: Oh, I see. I hadn't correctly divined your attitude towards your tenants. You see I mainly design slaughterhouses. Yes, pity. Mind you this is a real beaut. I mean, none of your blood caked on the walls and flesh flying out of the windows, inconveniencing passers-by with this one. I mean, my life has been building up to this.

SECOND CITY GENT: Yes, and well done. But we did want a block of flats.

MR WIGGIN: Well, may I ask you to reconsider? I mean, you wouldn't regret it. Think of the tourist trade.

FIRST CITY GENT: No, no, it's just that we wanted a block of flats, not an abattoir.

MR WIGGIN: Yes, well, of course, that's just the sort of blinkered philistine pig ignorance I've come to expect from you non-creative garbage. You sit there on your loathsome, spotty behinds squeezing blackheads, not caring a tinker's cuss about the struggling artist. *(shouting)* You excrement! You lousy hypocritical whining toadies with your lousy colour TV sets and your Tony Jacklin golf clubs and your bleeding masonic handshakes! You wouldn't let me join, would you, you blackballing bastards! Well I wouldn't become a freemason now if you went down on your lousy, stinking, purulent knees and begged me.

SECOND CITY GENT: Well, we're sorry you feel like that but we, er, did want a block of flats. Nice though the abattoir is.

MR WIGGIN: Oh *(blows raspberry)* the abattoir, that's not important. But if one of you could put in a word for me I'd love to be a freemason. Freemasonry opens doors. I mean, I was . . . I was a bit on edge just now, but if I was a mason I'd just sit at the back and not get in anyone's way.

FIRST CITY GENT: Thank you.

MR WIGGIN: I've got a second-hand apron.

SECOND CITY GENT: Thank you.

MR WIGGIN *(going to the door but stopping)*: I nearly got in at Hendon.

FIRST CITY GENT: Thank you.

NEVER BE RUDE TO AN ARAB

a plea for tolerance and understanding
(in a world full of fucking loonies)

Never be rude to an Arab,
An Israeli, or Saudi, or Jew,
Never be rude to an Irishman
No matter what you do.
Never poke fun at a Nigger,
A Spik, or a Wop, or a Kraut,
And never put DOWN . . .

THE
MARTYRDOM
OF ST BRIAN

And it came to pass that St Brian was taken from his place to another place where he was lain upon pillows of silk and made to rest himself amongst sheets of muslin and velvet, and there stroked was he by maidens of the Orient. Full sixteen days and nights stroked they him, yea verily and caressed him. His hair ruffled they and their fingers rubbed they in oil of olives and ran them across all parts of his body forasmuch as to soothe him. And the soles of his feet licked they and the upper parts of his thigh did they anoint with the balm of forbidden trees, and with the teeth of their mouths nibbled they the pointed bits at the top of his ears, yea verily and did their tongues thereof make themselves acquainted with his secret places. For fifteen days and nights did Brian withstand these maidens, but on the sixteenth day he cried out, saying: "This is fantastic!" "Oh! this is terrific!" And the Lord did hear the cry of Brian and verily he came down and slew the maidens and their jars of oil tipped he over and he caused their cotton wool to blow away. Then he sent down seven dark stallions carrying seven mighty warriors who did breathe fire about the place where Brian had lain, so the soft furnishings thereof perished – and Brian carried he up amongst the clouds to remain with him forever. And Brian in his anguish cried out that the Lord was a rotten bastard, but the Lord heard his cry and forgave He him and Brian did rest with the angels.

But it came to pass that Brian's fingers could not be still, and male and female poked he them. And the angel of the Lord saw that Brian's fingers were full of naughtiness, and he spake unto Brian, saying: "Thy fingers are full of naughtiness and they have become like unto great big adders in the sight of the Lord." And Brian knew that his fingers had sinned, and he went unto an high place and was ashamed. And the angel of the Lord came to Brian and laid his arm upon him and spake unto him: "Fear not Brian, for if thou eschew thy fingers and the naughtiness thereof – get off – yea verily shall the Lord see that thou hast indeed been sore tempted but have from this day forward ceased to sin." And Brian eschewed his fingers and the use thereof for evermore, apart from odd occasions, and he was from that day forward blest in the sight of the Lord, and his name was called Saint Brian, and he dwelt amongst the Heavenly Host from that day forward.

MR CREOSOTE

MAÎTRE D: Ah good afternoon, sir, and how are we today?

MR CREOSOTE: Better . . .

MAÎTRE D: Better?

MR CREOSOTE: Better get a bucket, I'm going to throw up.

MAÎTRE D: Gaston! A bucket for monsieur!

They seat him at his usual table. A gleaming silver bucket is placed beside him and he leans over and throws up into it.

MAÎTRE D: Merci Gaston.

He claps his hands and the bucket is whisked away.

MR CREOSOTE: I haven't finished!

MAÎTRE D: Oh! Pardon! Gaston! . . . A thousand pardons monsieur. *(He puts the bucket back)*

The MAÎTRE D *produces the menu as* MR CREOSOTE *continues spewing.*

MAÎTRE D: Now this afternoon we have monsieur's favourite – the jugged hare. The hare is *very* high, and the sauce is very rich with truffles, anchovies, Grand Marnier, bacon and cream.

MR CREOSOTE *pauses. The* MAÎTRE D *claps his hands and signs to* GASTON, *who whisks away the bucket.*

MAÎTRE D: Thank you, Gaston.

MR CREOSOTE: There's still more.

GASTON *rapidly replaces the bucket.*

MAÎTRE D: Allow me! A new bucket for monsieur.

The MAÎTRE D *picks the bucket up and hands it over to* GASTON.

MR CREOSOTE *leans over and throws up on to the floor.*

And maintenant, would monsieur care for an apéritif?

MR CREOSOTE *vomits over the menu.*

Or would you prefer to order straight away? Today we have for appetizers . . . er . . . excuse me . . .

MAÎTRE D: . . . moules marinières, pâté de foie gras, beluga caviar, eggs Benedictine, tarte de poireaux – that's leek tart – frogs' legs amandine or oeufs de caille Richard Shepherd – c'est à dire, little quails' eggs on a bed of puréed mushrooms, it's very delicate, very subtle . . .

MR CREOSOTE: I'll have the lot.

MAÎTRE D: A wise choice, monsieur! And now, how would you like it served? All mixed up in a bucket?

MR CREOSOTE: Yes. With the eggs on top.

MAÎTRE D: But of course, avec les oeufs frites.

MR CREOSOTE: And don't skimp on the pâté.

MAÎTRE D: Oh monsieur I can assure you, just because it is mixed up with all the other things we would not dream of giving you less than the full amount. In fact I will personally make sure you have a *double* helping. Maintenant quelque chose à boire – something to drink, monsieur?

MR CREOSOTE: Yeah, six bottles of Château Latour '45 and a double Jeroboam of champagne.

MAÎTRE D: Bon, and the usual brown ales . . .?

MR CREOSOTE: Yeah . . . No wait a minute . . . I think I could only manage six crates today.

MAÎTRE D: Tut tut tut! I hope monsieur was not overdoing it last night . . .?

MR CREOSOTE: Shut up!

MAÎTRE D: D'accord. Ah the new bucket and the cleaning woman.

GASTON *arrives. The* CLEANING WOMAN *gets down on her hands and knees.* MR CREOSOTE *vomits over her.*

52

Some guests at another table start to leave. The MAÎTRE D *approaches.*

MAÎTRE D: Monsieur, is there something wrong with the food?

The MAÎTRE D *indicates the table of half-eaten main courses. The guests shrink from his vomit-covered hand. The* MAÎTRE D *realises and shakes a little off. It hits another guest, who wipes his eye.*

GUEST: No. The food was . . . excellent . . .

They start to go. The MAÎTRE D *follows.*

MAÎTRE D: Thank you so much, so nice to see you and I hope very much we will see you again very soon. Au revoir, monsieur.

He pauses. A look of awful realization suffuses his face.

MAÎTRE D: . . . Oh dear . . . I've trodden in monsieur's bucket.

The MAÎTRE D *claps his hands.*

Another bucket for monsieur . . .

MR CREOSOTE *is sick down the* MAÎTRE D*'s trousers.*

and perhaps a hose . . .

Someone at another table gently throws up.

COMPANION: Oh Max, really!

Meanwhile MR CREOSOTE *has scoffed the lot. The* MAÎTRE D *approaches him with a silver tray.*

MAÎTRE D: And finally, monsieur, a wafer-thin mint.

MR CREOSOTE: No.

MAÎTRE D: Oh sir! It's only a tiny little one.

MR CREOSOTE: No. Fuck off – I'm full . . . *(Belches)*

MAÎTRE D: Oh sir . . . it's only *wafer* thin.

MR CREOSOTE: Look – I couldn't eat another thing. I'm absolutely stuffed. Bugger off.

MAÎTRE D: Oh sir, just . . . just *one* . . .

MR CREOSOTE: Oh all right. Just one.

MAÎTRE D: Just the one, sir . . . voilà . . . bon appétit . . .

MR CREOSOTE *somehow manages to stuff the wafer-thin mint into his mouth and then swallows. The* MAÎTRE D *takes a flying leap and cowers behind some potted plants. There is an ominous splitting sound.* MR CREOSOTE *looks rather helpless and then he explodes.*

$TOCK
MARKET REPORT

Trading was crisp at the start of the day with some brisk business on the floor. Rubber hardened and string remained confident. Little bits of tin consolidated although biscuits sank after an early gain and stools remained anonymous. Armpits rallied well after a poor start. Nipples rose dramatically during the morning but had declined by mid-afternoon, while teeth clenched and buttocks remained firm. Small dark furry things increased severely on the floor, whilst rude jellies wobbled up and down, and bounced against rising thighs which had spread to all parts of the country by mid-afternoon. After lunch naughty things dipped sharply, forcing giblets upwards. Ting tang tong rankled dithely, little tipples pooped and poppy things went pong!

56

NOVEL WRITING
LIVE FROM DORCHESTER

COMMENTATOR: Hello and welcome to Dorchester where a very good crowd has turned out to watch local boy Thomas Hardy write his new novel, *The Return of the Native*, on this very pleasant July morning. And here he comes!

Here comes Hardy walking out towards his desk. He looks confident, he looks relaxed, very much the man in form, as he acknowledges this very good-natured bank holiday crowd . . .

And the crowd goes quiet now as Hardy settles himself down at the desk. Body straight . . . shoulders relaxed . . . pen held lightly but firmly in the right hand . . . the second finger coming round just underneath the base of the pen . . . he dips the pen in the ink . . . And he's off! And it's the first word! But it's not a word! Oh no! It's a doodle way up on the top of the left hand margin. It's a piece of meaningless scribble . . . and he's signed his name underneath it, oh dear, what a disappointing start . . . But he's off again! Yes there he goes – the first word of Thomas Hardy's new novel at 10.35 on this very lovely morning – it's three letters, it's the definite article and it's "The" . . . Richie Benaud.

RICHIE: Well this is true to form. No surprise there. He's started five of his eleven novels to date with the definite article, we've had two of them with "It", there's been one "But", two "Ats" and one "On" and a "Dolores", though that, of course, was never published.

COMMENTATOR: I'm sorry to interrupt you there, Richie, but he's crossed it out. Thomas Hardy here on the first day of his new novel has crossed out the only word he's written so far, and he's gazing off into space . . . But no, he's off and writing again . . . and yes: he's written "The" again! He's crossed it out again! That's twice he's written the definite article and twice he's crossed it out! And what's the replacement? It's . . . the indefinite article! This great novelist has replaced the definite article with the indefinite article, and there's a second word coming up straight away . . . no pause for thought . . . and it's "Sat" . . .

"A Sat . . ." doesn't make sense . . . "A Satur . . ." "A Saturday"! it's "A Saturday" and the crowd are loving it! They're really enjoying this novel. And it's "afternoon" . . . "A Saturday afternoon" . . . It's a confident beginning . . . And he's straight on to the next word . . . it's "in" . . . "A Saturday afternoon in . . . in . . . in . . . in . . . Novembr!" November spelt wrong . . . he's left out the second "e" . . . but he's not going back! It looks as though he's going to go for the sentence! And it's the first verb coming up! It's the first verb of the novel . . . and it's "was"! And the crowd are going wild! "A Saturday afternoon in November was . . ." and a long word here . . . "appro . . ." is it "approval"? No! It's "approaching"! "A Saturday afternoon in November was approaching" and he's done the definite article, "the", again, and he's writing fluently, easily, with flowing strokes of his pen, as he comes up to the middle of this first sentence . . . and with this eleventh novel well under way and the prospects of a good day's writing ahead, back to the studio.

THE KNIGHTS WHO SAY
'NI'

Big close-up of a frightening black-browed evil face.

TALL KNIGHT: Ni!

KING ARTHUR *and* SIR BEDEVERE *recoil in abject fear.* PATSY *rears up with coconuts.*

ARTHUR: Easy . . . boy, easy . . .

(He peers into the darkness.)

Who are you?

SIX VOICES FROM THE DARKNESS: Ni! . . . Peng! . . . Neeee . . . Wom!

An extraordinarily TALL KNIGHT *all in black looms out of the darkness. He is extremely fierce and of gruesome countenance.*

ARTHUR: Who are you?

TALL KNIGHT: We are the Knights Who Say "Ni"!

BEDEVERE *(in terror)*: No! Not the Knights Who Say "Ni"!

TALL KNIGHT: The same . . .

ARTHUR: Who are they?

TALL KNIGHT: We are the keepers of the Sacred Words. Ni . . . Peng . . . and Neee . . . Wom!

BEDEVERE: Those who hear them seldom live to tell the tale.

TALL KNIGHT: The Knights Who Say "Ni"! demand a sacrifice.

ARTHUR: Knights Who Say "Ni" . . . we are but simple travellers. We seek the Enchanter who lives beyond this wood and who . . .

TALL KNIGHT: Ni!

ARTHUR *(recoiling)*: Oh!

TALL KNIGHT: Ni! Ni!

ARTHUR *(he cowers in fear)*: Oh!

TALL KNIGHT: We shall say "Ni!" again if you do not appease us.

ARTHUR: All right! What do you want?

TALL KNIGHT: We want . . . a shrubbery!

ARTHUR: A *what*?

TALL KNIGHT: Ni! Ni! Ni . . . Peng . . . Nee . . . wom!

The PAGES *rear and snort and rattle their coconuts.*

ARTHUR: All right! All right! . . . no more, please. We will find you a shrubbery . . .

TALL KNIGHT: You must return here with a shrubbery or else . . . you shall not pass through this wood alive!

ARTHUR: Thank you, Knights Who Say Ni! You are fair and just. We will return with a shrubbery.

TALL KNIGHT: One that looks nice.

ARTHUR: Of course.

TALL KNIGHT: And not too expensive.

ARTHUR: Yes . . .

TALL KNIGHT: Now – go!

ARTHUR *and* BEDEVERE *turn and ride off. Shouts of* "Ni" *and* "Peng" *ring behind them.*

August 5th, 1974.

Dear Mike,

The Censor's representative, Tony Kerpel, came along to Friday's screening at Twickenham and he gave us his opinion of the film's probable certificate. He thinks the film will be AA, but it would be possible, given some dialogue cuts, to make the film an A rating, which would increase the audience. (AA is 14 and over, and A is 5 - 14).

For an "A" we would have to:

Lose as many *shits* as possible

Take *Jesus Christ* out, if possible

Lose "I fart in your general direction"

Lose "the *oral sex*"

Lose "oh, fuck off"

Lose "We make castanets out of your testicles"

I would like to get back to the Censor and agree to lose the *shits*, take the odd *Jesus Christ* out and lose *Oh fuck off*, but to retain "fart in your general direction", "castanets of your testicles" and "oral sex" and ask him for an "A" rating on that basis.

Please let me know as soon as possible your attitude to this.

Yours sincerely

Mark Forstater